Protein Power Smoothies:

30 Healthy & High-Protein Recipes for Every Lifestyle

By Shanele Regencia

Disclaimer

The information contained within this document is for educational and general informational purposes only.

All information in the book is provided in good faith and every reasonable effort has been made to ensure that the information provided is as accurate and complete as possible and free from errors; however, the author assumes no responsibility for errors, omissions, or contrary interpretation, and make no representation or warranty of any kind, express or implied, regarding the accuracy, adequacy, relevance, validity, reliability, availability, timeliness or completeness of any information on the book.

Under no circumstance shall we be held liable for any special, direct, indirect, consequential, or incidental loss or damage or any damages of any kind incurred because of the use of the book or reliance on any information provided in the book.

By using this book, you accept full personal responsibility for any harm or damage you suffer because of your actions arising out of or in connection with the use of the book.

You agree to use judgment and conduct due diligence to verify any information obtained from this book before taking any action or implementing any suggestions or recommendations set out on this book.

Your use of this book is solely at your own risk, and you expressly agree not to rely upon any information contained in this book.

We reserve the right to make additions, deletions, or modification to the contents on this book at any time without prior notice.

External links disclaimer

This book may contain links to external websites that are not provided or maintained by or in any way affiliated with us. This author does not guarantee the accuracy, adequacy, relevance, validity, reliability, availability, timeliness or completeness of any information on these external websites.

Medical Disclaimer

This book does not contain medical and health advice. The health information contained in this book is provided for general informational and educational purposes only and it is not intended as, and shall not be understood or construed as, professional medical advice, diagnosis, or treatment, or substitute for professional medical advice, diagnosis, or treatment.

Before taking any actions based upon such information, we expressly recommend that you seek advice from a medical professional.

Your use of this book is solely at your own risk, and you expressly agree not to rely upon any information contained in this book as a substitute for professional medical advice, diagnosis, or treatment.

Under no circumstance shall be held liable or responsible for any errors or omissions on this book or for any damage you may suffer in respect to any actions taken or not taken based on any or all the contents of this book and/or because of failing to seek competent advice from a medical professional.

Table of CONTENTS

Introduction

I have loved smoothies since high school!

Whether it was going out with family and friends or just needing a quick snack after a couple of hours shopping at the mall, smoothies were my go-to beverage. Back then, my teenage self cared less about the nutrients packed in this creamy, delicious drink. It just tasted great and felt refreshing, especially during the hot summer months in Tampa, Florida.

Then I started college, and smoothies became either my breakfast when I had morning classes or my snack in between classes. What was great about smoothies was that they were a simple on-the-go beverage, especially when I had to submit projects, term papers, and study for exams. Even after I graduated from college, I still buy smoothies from cafes.

But that changed in 2015. I had just completed a 5K race in the local area when I came across a stand that sold protein powders. As I was looking at the product, I learned that I could add them to my smoothies. Plus, buying premade smoothies or those made at cafes usually contained too much sugar and many calories. The benefit of making my own smoothies is that I can control what ingredients I put in. I can choose whatever fruit or vegetable I like, add protein powders or other additives such as honey and vanilla extract, and choose any liquid base, such as almond milk or water.

By controlling what ingredients to use, I can monitor how much sugar and how many calories are in the drink and adjust as necessary. So, I decided to give making my own smoothies a shot. And I'm glad I did. Nowadays, I make my own smoothies at home and sometimes bring them with me to work as my breakfast.

With that said, I hope you enjoy these 30 smoothie recipes and incorporating them into your daily lives.

Enjoy your smoothies!

Chapter 1

Health Benefits of Smoothies

Smoothies have long been popular among the health and wellness community and are one of the most frequently consumed health foods. These delicious treats can be enjoyed as a meal replacement, a pick-me-up snack, a dessert, or a post-workout drink. Smoothies often include a variety of healthy ingredients such as fruits, vegetables, nut butters, seeds, plant-based or dairy-free milk, and protein or collagen powders, just to name a few.

They are typically easy and quick to make, depending on the number of ingredients used. So, whether you need to quickly head to work or drop the kids off at school, blending a few ingredients together in a short time is a fantastic way to incorporate all those nutrients into your body.

So, what are smoothies?

Smoothies are thick, creamy beverages usually blended with puréed fruits, vegetables, juices, yogurt, nuts, seeds, and/or dairy or nondairy milk (Ld, 2020).

Since smoothies are diverse in textures and flavors, they are divided into the following well-known categories. Here are the three categories:

Fruit Smoothies: As name implies, these smoothies consist of different kinds of fruits mixed with either milk, water, juice, or ice cream.

Green Smoothies: These smoothies consist of green leafy vegetables and fruits blended with either milk, water, or juice. This beverage consists of mostly green leafy vegetables, but the fruits are added to add sweetness.

Protein Smoothies: Protein smoothies consist at least a fruit or vegetable mixed with a liquid and a protein source, such as Greek yogurt or a protein powder (Ld, 2020).

*However, in this recipe book, the categories are divided into vanilla and chocolate smoothies since all my recipes have **protein powder** as an ingredient.*

These smoothies are packed with various nutrients, vitamins, and minerals that are beneficial to not only to your physical health but also your overall well-being and quality of life. There are so many health benefits of smoothies but here are five awesome health benefits of incorporating these creamy beverages for a healthier you.

1. **More fruit and vegetable intake**

The World Health Organization (WHO) recommends that adults consume at least 5 servings (400g) of fruits and vegetables per day. Of course, many of us struggle to meet that daily requirement. Smoothies are a great way to help meet this daily recommendation because one serving of a smoothie can contain 2-3 servings of fruits and vegetables (Ld, 2020).

Smoothies are loaded with essential vitamins, minerals, fiber, and antioxidants. Your body quickly receives an abundance of these healthy nutrients, and they are easily digested. So, if you are having a tough time consuming 5 servings of fruits and vegetables a day, drinking a smoothie can help you pack in 2-3 servings.

2. High Fiber Intake

Fiber is essential for gut health and provides nutrients for gut bacteria. Maintaining a healthy gut microbiome is important, as recent studies have shown that having a healthy gut microbiome can reduce the risk of inflammation and enhance the immune system. One of those studies show that adequate fiber intake reduced the risk of chronic illnesses, such as heart disease and type 2 diabetes (Quagliani & Felt-Gunderson, 2016).

So, how much fiber do you need to consume daily? According to United States Department of Agriculture (USDA), men need at least 38g of fiber and women at least 25g. For many of us, meeting that daily requirement can be a challenge. But drinking one smoothie a day can help with that if the ingredients are high in fiber. A high-fiber smoothie consists of fruits, vegetables, whole grains (oats), nuts, seeds, and legumes (such as beans) (Ld, 2020).

3. High Antioxidants

With all those fruits and vegetables blended in a smoothie, antioxidants are abundant and beneficial to your health. The great thing about antioxidants is that they prevent or delay cell damage, which is caused by free radicals. Free radicals, also known as reactive oxygen species (ROS), are unstable molecules that the body produces as a reaction to the environmental and other pressures (LD, 2023).

In other words, free radicals are just waste substances produced by your cells. It is important for your body to remove those waste substances to prevent oxidative stress since they are linked to many chronic diseases according to many studies. Chronic diseases can be heart disease, cancer, stroke, and Parkinson's disease, just to name a few (LD, 2023).

Antioxidants do that job removing free radicals. Think of them as "free radical scavengers." Our bodies do produce antioxidants to neutralize free radicals and those "free radical scavengers" are called endogenous antioxidants. However, our bodies depend more on external (exogenous), primarily the diet, to obtain the rest of the antioxidants it needs (*Antioxidants and Cancer Prevention*, 2017). These exogenous antioxidants are also known as dietary antioxidants.

Dietary antioxidants are found in many substances. Some of those substances are:

- Vitamin A
- Vitamin C
- Vitamin E
- Beta-carotene
- Lycopene
- Lutein (*Antioxidants and Cancer Prevention*, 2017).

Thus, smoothies are a great way to load yourself with many antioxidants that come from fruits and vegetables and sometimes protein powders. With protein powders, I advise that you check the brand, label, and do some research to see if the powder really does contain antioxidants. Yet, to be on the safe side, it is better to load yourself with antioxidants, mostly fruits and vegetables.

4. More Energy and Quick Post Workout Recovery

Yes, smoothies are loaded with nutrients that give you more energy and expedite muscle recovery after a long workout. Many athletes and those who work out often benefit from a post-workout smoothie because of its vitamins and minerals. The role of those large amounts of nutrients in a smoothie serving is that they lower inflammation, which results in decreasing soreness after a vigorous workout. The process of protein synthesis and repair is enhanced when the body has more protein post workout (Health Fitness Revolution, 2022).

Proteins are building blocks for our bodies, especially our muscles. When we workout, either lifting weights, power walking on a treadmill, or running a marathon, we put our muscles to work. During the workout, we developed wear and tears on our muscle due to strenuous demand. It is very important to replenish your body with protein so your body can quickly repair its muscles.

Smoothies are also great pre-workout drinks and a mid-afternoon pick-me-up. They provide fiber and carbohydrates the give you energy and keep you focused.

5. Strengthen Immune System

As mentioned in this chapter, smoothies enhance the immune system when your gut health is healthy. Early research suggests that a healthy, thriving community of gut bacteria can help reduce inflammation, promote healthy immune function, and support mental health (Ld, 2020). Your gut is where most of your immune system is.

Think of your gut microbiome as an immunity pharmacy (Juice Plus+, 2021). This "pharmacy" is a community of gut bugs. These gut bugs must work in a conducive environment to promote a healthy immune function. And what is that conducive environment? By feeding these gut bugs good food, such as fruits and vegetables. And that is where smoothies come in.

Despite being blended, fruits and vegetables still have the vitamins, minerals, and nutrients to keep the gut healthy for your immune system to be in excellent condition. A robust immune system can reduce symptoms of common ailments, such as colds and flu.

Summary

Smoothies are wonderful treats to consume due to their freshness and nutrition. Let's recap on the five health benefits of drinking smoothies:

- ✓ More fruit and vegetable intake
- ✓ High fiber intake
- ✓ High antioxidants
- ✓ More energy and quick post-workout recovery
- ✓ Strengthen immune system

There are many other health benefits of smoothies, but these are just some of it. You can learn more about those benefits by checking the reference section in the end of the book.

Chapter 2

Smoothie Basics

Now that you know about the great health benefits, it's time to make a smoothie! Many of us already know how to make a smoothie by reading recipe books, magazines, or online content. However, we often use our blenders and measuring cups and spoons without understanding the basics.

In this chapter, you will learn about the essential ingredients of a smoothie and tips on how to make one *without dirtying your kitchen or spending extra time cleaning up afterward.*

Smoothie's Basic Ingredients

Smoothies are known for their creamy consistency and texture. Whether you create your own smoothies or buy one at your local smoothie place or grocery store, the most delicious smoothie always has that creamy and slightly thick texture.

You can taste all the main ingredients, and it feels great to know that you're getting all those nutrients from just one smoothie. To achieve that creamy, slightly thick texture, you need to know the three main ingredients. Once you understand how these ingredients work, you can get creative in mixing them. So now, let us discuss each ingredient.

1. Liquid Base

The foundation of smoothies is liquid. A smoothie is not a smoothie without a liquid base. You can use any liquids, such as milk, fresh juice (not referring to the store juice), or just water. Mineral water is the simplest liquid base and adding this ingredient can give the smoothie that airy texture.

Water-based smoothies are not necessarily bland and plain. You can add some sweetness by adding a sweet fruit or if you want a low-calorie beverage, then add a vegetable. You will still taste the flavor or either that fruit or vegetable.

2. Base Ingredients

The two main base ingredients are fruits and vegetables. While the liquid base provides consistency, these ingredients contribute the primary flavor. Fruit-based smoothies are usually sweet due to the natural sugar content of the fruits, whereas vegetable-based smoothies are rich in fiber.

3. Natural Additives

These additives enhance the flavor, taste, and quality of the smoothie. Examples include seeds, protein powders, nut butters, and toppings.

Tips on How to Prepare a Smoothie (without dirtying your kitchen and spending extra time cleaning up

Whether it's shortly after an intensive workout or just as a snack, I prepare a smoothie with my favorite ingredients. By combining the three main components mentioned above, it is quick to put together and ready to consume. Here are some general tips on how to prepare a smoothie.

1. Begin with the produce. For fruit smoothies, I add about 1/2 to 1 cup of fresh fruits. For vegetable smoothies, I add 1 to 3 fresh vegetables. For a creamier texture and consistency, freeze your fruits and vegetables before putting them in the blender. Smoothies are more delicious and richer when they are frozen!

2. Then add the wet ingredients. For a creamier texture, use any type of milk, whether nut-based, skim, or whole milk. Sometimes, if I want more vanilla flavor in my smoothie, I add about a teaspoon of vanilla extract.

   I also try other extracts to add different flavors. For example, if I want to make a chocolate peppermint smoothie, I add about 1/8 teaspoon of peppermint extract. You can add any extracts you like.

   Notice that I do not add the wet ingredients first. If you pour those ingredients first, the liquid will splash on the counter when you add the fruits and vegetables afterward. So, it is important to add the produce before the wet ingredients.

3. Add the dry ingredients. Dry ingredients refer to natural additives, such as protein powders and nut butters.

4. Add ice. After blending all the ingredients mentioned in the previous steps, then add ice.

   NOTE:

   a. **If the fruits or vegetables are frozen, there is no need to add ice.**
   b. *If Greek yogurt is one of the ingredients, freeze it before combining it with the other ingredients. That would replace the ice.*

5. Blend again and serve. *NOTE: If fruits or vegetables are frozen, then there is no need to blend twice.*

The next two chapters consist of different recipes for smoothies. Since many of the recipes are mixed with fruits and vegetables, the chapters are divided into chocolate and vanilla protein smoothies.

Enjoying these 30 high-protein smoothie recipes!

Chapter 3

Vanilla Protein Smoothie Recipes

Vanilla protein powder and vanilla extract are the main additives in these 15 delightful vanilla smoothie recipes. These two ingredients blend with various others, imparting a rich and inviting vanilla flavor to each smoothie. While many vanilla smoothies typically feature fruits, vegetables, or a mix of both, I've also included some unique recipes that forgo these components. Instead, I've chosen to use frozen vanilla Greek yogurt to create a creamy and thick texture, ensuring those smoothies are just as delicious without fruit or vegetables.

So, without further ado, let's dive into these 15 irresistible vanilla smoothie recipes and enjoy the smooth, velvety goodness in every sip!

Strawberry Pineapple Protein Smoothie

Prep Time: 10 minutes
Serving: 1

Shopping List:

- ✓ Plant-based milk (i.e., almond, coconut)
- ✓ Strawberries
- ✓ Pineapple
- ✓ Vanilla Protein Powder
- ✓ Vanilla Extract

Ingredients:

- 1 cup plant-based milk
- ½ cup strawberries, frozen
- ½ cup pineapple, in chunks, frozen
- 1 scoop of vanilla protein powder
- 1 tsp vanilla extract

Directions:

1. Combine all ingredients in a blender.
2. Blend all ingredients until smoothie is thick and creamy.
3. Serve and enjoy!

NOTE:

- It is better to use frozen fruits for a rich, thicker and creamier texture.
- In case you do not have frozen fruits available, then add 1 cup of ice.
- Follow "Tips on How to Prepare a Smoothie (without dirtying your kitchen and spending extra time cleaning up" at the end of Chapter 2.

PROTEIN POWER SMOOTHIES

Mixed Berry Protein Smoothie

Prep Time: 10 minutes
Serving: 1

Shopping List:

- ✓ Plant-based milk (i.e., almond, coconut)
- ✓ Strawberries
- ✓ Blueberries
- ✓ Raspberries or Blackberries
- ✓ Vanilla Protein Powder
- ✓ Vanilla Extract

Ingredients:

- 1 cup plant-based milk
- ½ cup strawberries, in halves
- ½ cup blueberries
- ¼ cup raspberries (or blackberries)
- 1 scoop of vanilla protein powder
- 1 tsp vanilla extract

Directions:

1. Combine all ingredients in a blender
2. Blend all ingredients until smoothie is thick and creamy
3. Serve and enjoy!

NOTE:

- *May substitute 1 cup of mixed berry combination instead of measuring each berry individually.*
- It is better to use frozen fruits for a rich, thicker and creamier texture.
- In case you do not have frozen fruits available, then add 1 cup of ice.

- Follow "Tips on How to Prepare a Smoothie (without dirtying your kitchen and spending extra time cleaning up" at the end of Chapter 2.

Plain Vanilla Protein Smoothie

Prep Time: 10 minutes
Serving: 1

Shopping List:

- ✓ Plant-based milk (i.e., almond, coconut)
- ✓ Vanilla Greek Yogurt
- ✓ Vanilla Protein Powder
- ✓ Vanilla Extract

Ingredients:

- 1 cup plant-based milk
- 1 scoop of vanilla protein powder
- 1 tsp vanilla extract
- ½ cup vanilla Greek yogurt, frozen

Directions:

1. Combine all ingredients in a blender
2. Blend all ingredients until smoothie is thick and creamy
3. Serve and enjoy!

NOTE:

- *Freeze the Greek yogurt before combining it with the other ingredients. That would replace the ice.*
- Frozen Greek yogurt makes this Vanilla Protein Smoothie thicker and creamier.
- You do not have to freeze the dates.
- Follow "Tips on How to Prepare a Smoothie (without dirtying your kitchen and spending extra time cleaning up" at the end of Chapter 2.

Honey Dates Vanilla Protein Smoothie

Prep Time: 10 minutes
Serving: 1

Shopping List:

- ✓ Plant-based milk (i.e., almond, coconut)
- ✓ Pitted Dates
- ✓ Honey
- ✓ Frozen Vanilla Greek Yogurt
- ✓ Vanilla Protein Powder
- ✓ Vanilla Extract

Ingredients:

- 1 cup plant-based milk (I use almond, coconut, or both)
- 3 dates, pitted
- ½ cup frozen vanilla Greek yogurt
- 1 scoop of vanilla protein powder
- 1tsp vanilla extract
- ½ tbsp honey

Directions:

1. Combine all ingredients in a blender.
2. Blend all ingredients until smoothie is thick and creamy.
3. Serve and enjoy!

NOTE:

- *Freeze the Greek yogurt before combining it with the other ingredients. That would replace the ice.*
- Frozen Greek yogurt makes this Vanilla Protein Smoothie thicker and creamier.

- Follow "Tips on How to Prepare a Smoothie (without dirtying your kitchen and spending extra time cleaning up" at the end of Chapter 2.

Banana Clementine Protein Smoothie

Prep Time: 10 minutes
Serving: 1

Shopping List:

- ✓ Plant-based milk (i.e., almond, coconut)
- ✓ Frozen Banana
- ✓ Frozen Clementines
- ✓ Vanilla Protein Powder
- ✓ Vanilla Extract

Ingredients:

- 1 cup plant-based milk
- 1 banana, frozen
- 2 clementines, frozen
- 1 scoop of vanilla protein powder
- 1 tsp vanilla extract

Directions:

1. Combine all ingredients in a blender.
2. Blend all ingredients until smoothie is thick and creamy.
3. Serve and enjoy!

NOTE:

- It is better to use frozen fruits for a rich, thicker and creamier texture.
- In case you do not have frozen fruits available, then add 1 cup of ice.
- Follow "Tips on How to Prepare a Smoothie (without dirtying your kitchen and spending extra time cleaning up" at the end of Chapter 2.

Banana Protein Smoothie

Prep Time: 10 minutes
Serving: 1

Shopping List:

- ✓ Plant-based milk (i.e., almond, coconut)
- ✓ Frozen Banana
- ✓ Vanilla Protein Powder
- ✓ Vanilla Extract

Ingredients:

- 1 cup plant-based milk
- 1 banana, frozen
- 1 scoop of vanilla protein powder
- 1 tsp vanilla extract

Directions:

1. Combine all ingredients in a blender.
2. Blend all ingredients until smoothie is thick and creamy.
3. Serve and enjoy!

NOTE:

- It is better to use frozen fruits for a rich, thicker and creamier texture.
- In case you do not have frozen fruits available, then add 1 cup of ice.
- Follow "Tips on How to Prepare a Smoothie (without dirtying your kitchen and spending extra time cleaning up" at the end of Chapter 2.

Strawberry Protein Smoothie

Prep Time: 10 minutes
Serving: 1

Shopping List:

- ✓ Plant-based milk (i.e., almond, coconut)
- ✓ Frozen Strawberries
- ✓ Vanilla Protein Powder
- ✓ Vanilla Extract

Ingredients:

- 1 cup plant-based milk
- 1 cup strawberries, in halves & frozen
- 1 scoop of vanilla protein powder
- 1 tsp vanilla extract

Directions:

1. Combine all ingredients in a blender.
2. Blend all ingredients until smoothie is thick and creamy.
3. Serve and enjoy!

NOTE:

- It is better to use frozen fruits for a rich, thicker and creamier texture.
- In case you do not have frozen fruits available, then add 1 cup of ice.
- Follow "Tips on How to Prepare a Smoothie (without dirtying your kitchen and spending extra time cleaning up" at the end of Chapter 2.

Banana and Dates Protein Smoothie

Prep Time: 10 minutes
Serving: 1

Shopping List:

- ✓ Plant-based milk (i.e., almond, coconut)
- ✓ Pitted Dates
- ✓ Frozen Banana
- ✓ Vanilla Protein Powder
- ✓ Vanilla Extract

Ingredients:

- 1 cup plant-based milk
- 3 dates, non-pitted
- 1 banana, medium
- 1 scoop of vanilla protein powder
- 1 tsp vanilla extract

Directions:

1. Combine all ingredients in a blender.
2. Blend all ingredients until smoothie is thick and creamy.
3. Serve and enjoy!

NOTE:

- It is better to use frozen fruits for a rich, thicker and creamier texture.
- In case you do not have frozen fruits available, then add 1 cup of ice.
- Follow "Tips on How to Prepare a Smoothie (without dirtying your kitchen and spending extra time cleaning up" at the end of Chapter 2.

Blueberry Protein Smoothie

Prep Time: 10 minutes
Serving: 1

Shopping List:

- ✓ Plant-based milk (i.e., almond, coconut)
- ✓ Frozen Blueberries
- ✓ Vanilla Protein Powder
- ✓ Vanilla Extract

Ingredients:

- 1 cup plant-based milk
- 1 cup blueberries
- 1 scoop of vanilla protein powder
- 1 tsp vanilla extract

Directions:

1. Combine all ingredients in a blender.
2. Blend all ingredients until smoothie is thick and creamy.
3. Serve and enjoy!

NOTE:

- It is better to use frozen fruits for a rich, thicker and creamier texture.
- In case you do not have frozen fruits available, then add 1 cup of ice.
- Follow "Tips on How to Prepare a Smoothie (without dirtying your kitchen and spending extra time cleaning up" at the end of Chapter 2.

Vanilla Honey Protein Smoothie

Prep Time: 10 minutes
Serving: 1

Shopping List:

- ✓ Plant-based milk (i.e., almond, coconut)
- ✓ Frozen Vanilla Greek Yogurt
- ✓ Vanilla Protein Powder
- ✓ Honey
- ✓ Vanilla Extract

Ingredients:

- 1 cup plant-based milk
- ½ cup frozen vanilla Greek Yogurt
- 1 scoop of vanilla protein powder
- 1 tbsp honey
- 1 tsp vanilla extract

Directions:

1. Combine all ingredients in a blender.
2. Blend all ingredients until smoothie is thick and creamy.
3. Serve and enjoy!

NOTE:

- *Freeze the Greek yogurt before combining it with the other ingredients. That would replace the ice.*
- Frozen Greek yogurt makes this Vanilla Protein Smoothie thicker and creamier.
- Follow "Tips on How to Prepare a Smoothie (without dirtying your kitchen and spending extra time cleaning up" at the end of Chapter 2.

Strawberry Banana Protein Smoothie

Prep Time: 10 minutes
Serving: 1

Shopping List:

- ✓ Plant-based milk (i.e., almond, coconut)
- ✓ Frozen Strawberries
- ✓ Frozen Banana
- ✓ Vanilla Protein Powder
- ✓ Vanilla Extract

Ingredients:

- 1 ¼ cup plant-based milk
- 1 cup strawberries, in halves & frozen
- 1 banana, frozen
- 1 scoop of vanilla protein powder
- 1 tsp vanilla extract

Directions:

1. Combine all ingredients in a blender.
2. Blend all ingredients until smoothie is thick and creamy.
3. Serve and enjoy!

NOTE:

- It is better to use frozen fruits for a rich, thicker and creamier texture.
- In case you do not have frozen fruits available, then add 1 cup of ice.
- Follow "Tips on How to Prepare a Smoothie (without dirtying your kitchen and spending extra time cleaning up" at the end of Chapter 2.

Green Protein Smoothie

Prep Time: 10 minutes
Serving: 1

Shopping List:

- ✓ Plant-based milk (i.e., almond, coconut)
- ✓ Spinach (or Kale)
- ✓ Frozen Banana
- ✓ Vanilla Protein Powder
- ✓ Vanilla Extract

Ingredients:

- 1 cup plant-based milk
- 1 banana, frozen
- 3 cups spinach (or kale)
- 1 scoop of vanilla protein powder
- 1 tsp vanilla extract

Directions:

1. Combine all ingredients in a blender.
2. Blend all ingredients until smoothie is thick and creamy.
3. Serve and enjoy!

NOTE:

- *Spinach or Kale does not need to be frozen. The frozen banana will make up for it.*
- *In case the Green Smoothie is not cold, just some ice.*
- It is better to use frozen fruits for a rich, thicker and creamier texture.
- In case you do not have frozen fruits available, then add 1 cup of ice.

- Follow "Tips on How to Prepare a Smoothie (without dirtying your kitchen and spending extra time cleaning up" at the end of Chapter 2.

Banana Honey Protein Smoothie

Prep Time: 10 minutes
Serving: 1

Shopping List:

- ✓ Plant-based milk (i.e., almond, coconut)
- ✓ Frozen Banana
- ✓ Vanilla Protein Powder
- ✓ Vanilla Extract
- ✓ Honey

Ingredients:

- 1 cup plant-based milk
- 1 banana, frozen
- 1 scoop of vanilla protein powder
- 1 tsp vanilla extract
- ½ tbsp honey

Directions:

1. Combine all ingredients in a blender.
2. Blend all ingredients until smoothie is thick and creamy.
3. Serve and enjoy!

NOTE:

- It is better to use frozen fruits for a rich, thicker and creamier texture.
- In case you do not have frozen fruits available, then add 1 cup of ice.
- Follow "Tips on How to Prepare a Smoothie (without dirtying your kitchen and spending extra time cleaning up" at the end of Chapter 2.

Mango Banana Protein Smoothie

Prep Time: 10 minutes
Serving: 1

Shopping List:

- ✓ Plant-based milk (i.e., almond, coconut)
- ✓ Frozen Mango
- ✓ Frozen Banana
- ✓ Vanilla Protein Powder
- ✓ Vanilla Extract

Ingredients:

- 1 cup plant-based milk
- 1 mango, frozen
- 1 banana, frozen
- 1 scoop of vanilla protein powder
- 1 tsp vanilla extract

Directions:

1. Combine all ingredients in a blender.
2. Blend all ingredients until smoothie is thick and creamy.
3. Serve and enjoy!

NOTE:

- It is better to use frozen fruits for a rich, thicker and creamier texture.
- In case you do not have frozen fruits available, then add 1 cup of ice.
- Follow "Tips on How to Prepare a Smoothie (without dirtying your kitchen and spending extra time cleaning up" at the end of Chapter 2.

Cinnamon Apple Protein Smoothie

Prep Time: 10 minutes
Serving: 1

Shopping List:

- ✓ Plant-based milk (i.e., almond, coconut)
- ✓ Frozen Apple
- ✓ Vanilla Protein Powder
- ✓ Cinnamon
- ✓ Vanilla Extract

Ingredients:

- 1 cup plant-based milk
- 1 apple
- 1 tsp cinnamon
- 1 scoop of vanilla protein powder
- 1 tsp vanilla extract

Directions:

1. Combine all ingredients in a blender.
2. Blend all ingredients until smoothie is thick and creamy.
3. Serve and enjoy!

NOTE:

- It is better to use frozen fruits for a rich, thicker and creamier texture.
- In case you do not have frozen fruits available, then add 1 cup of ice.
- Follow "Tips on How to Prepare a Smoothie (without dirtying your kitchen and spending extra time cleaning up" at the end of Chapter 2.

Chapter 4

Chocolate Protein Smoothie Recipes

In this chapter, chocolate protein powder and cocoa powder are the main ingredients in these 15 decadent chocolate smoothies. These two elements are crucial for delivering that rich, chocolatey taste you crave.

Much like the vanilla smoothies, when fruits, vegetables, or a combination of both are not included, I've opted to use Greek yogurt to achieve the desired creamy texture. Specifically, I've chosen frozen chocolate Greek yogurt. If chocolate yogurt isn't available, frozen plain Greek yogurt (without vanilla) serves as a perfect alternative.

So go ahead and indulge in these 15 delicious chocolate smoothies, and savor their rich, chocolatey texture!

Double Chocolate Peanut Butter Protein Smoothie

Prep Time: 10 minutes
Serving: 1

Shopping List:

- ✓ Plant-based milk (i.e., almond, coconut)
- ✓ Peanut Butter
- ✓ Chocolate Protein Powder
- ✓ Chocolate Greek Yogurt
- ✓ Cocoa Powder

Ingredients:

- 1 cup plant-based milk
- 1 tbsp peanut butter
- 1 scoop of chocolate protein powder
- ½ cup chocolate Greek yogurt, frozen
- 1 tbsp cocoa powder

Directions:

1. Combine all ingredients in a blender.
2. Blend all ingredients until smoothie is thick and creamy.
3. Serve and enjoy!

NOTE:

- *Freeze the Greek yogurt before combining it with the other ingredients. That would replace the ice.*
- Frozen Greek yogurt makes this protein smoothie thicker and creamier.
- May substitute peanut butter for peanut butter powder.

- Follow "Tips on How to Prepare a Smoothie (without dirtying your kitchen and spending extra time cleaning up" at the end of Chapter 2.

Chocolate Peanut Butter Protein Smoothie

Prep Time: 10 minutes
Serving: 1

Shopping List:

- ✓ Plant-based milk (i.e., almond, coconut)
- ✓ Peanut Butter
- ✓ Chocolate Protein Powder
- ✓ Plain Greek Yogurt
- ✓ Cocoa Powder

Ingredients:

- 1 cup plant-based milk
- 1 tbsp peanut butter
- 1 scoop of chocolate protein powder
- ½ cup plain Greek yogurt, frozen
- 1 tbsp cocoa powder

Directions:

1. Combine all ingredients in a blender.
2. Blend all ingredients until smoothie is thick and creamy.
3. Serve and enjoy!

NOTE:

- *Freeze the Greek yogurt before combining it with the other ingredients. That would replace the ice.*
- Frozen Greek yogurt makes this protein smoothie thicker and creamier.
- May substitute peanut butter for peanut butter powder.
- Follow "Tips on How to Prepare a Smoothie (without dirtying your kitchen and spending extra time cleaning up" at the end of Chapter 2.

Chocolate Protein Smoothie

Prep Time: 10 minutes
Serving: 1

Shopping List:

- ✓ Plant-based milk (i.e., almond, coconut)
- ✓ Chocolate Protein Powder
- ✓ Plain Greek Yogurt
- ✓ Cocoa Powder

Ingredients:

- 1 cup plant-based milk
- ½ cup plain Greek yogurt
- 1 scoop of chocolate protein powder
- 1 tbsp cocoa powder

Directions:

1. Combine all ingredients in a blender.
2. Blend all ingredients until smoothie is thick and creamy.
3. Serve and enjoy!

NOTE:

- *Freeze the Greek yogurt before combining it with the other ingredients. That would replace the ice.*
- Frozen Greek yogurt makes this protein smoothie thicker and creamier.
- Follow "Tips on How to Prepare a Smoothie (without dirtying your kitchen and spending extra time cleaning up" at the end of Chapter 2.

Double Chocolate Protein Smoothie

Prep Time: 10 minutes
Serving: 1

Shopping List:

- ✓ Plant-based milk (i.e., almond, coconut)
- ✓ Chocolate Protein Powder
- ✓ Chocolate Greek Yogurt
- ✓ Cocoa Powder

Ingredients:

- 1 cup plant-based milk
- ½ cup Chocolate Greek yogurt
- 1 scoop of chocolate protein powder
- 1 tbsp cocoa powder

Directions:

1. Combine all ingredients in a blender.
2. Blend all ingredients until smoothie is thick and creamy.
3. Serve and enjoy!

NOTE:

- *Freeze the Greek yogurt before combining it with the other ingredients. That would replace the ice.*
- Frozen Greek yogurt makes this protein smoothie thicker and creamier.
- Follow "Tips on How to Prepare a Smoothie (without dirtying your kitchen and spending extra time cleaning up" at the end of Chapter 2.

Chocolate Peanut Butter Banana Protein Smoothie

Prep Time: 10 minutes
Serving: 1

Shopping List:

- ✓ Plant-based milk (i.e., almond, coconut)
- ✓ Peanut Butter
- ✓ Banana
- ✓ Chocolate Protein Powder
- ✓ Cocoa Powder

Ingredients:

- 1 cup plant-based milk
- 1 tbsp peanut butter
- 1 banana, medium
- 1 scoop of chocolate protein powder
- 1 tbsp cocoa powder

Directions:

1. Combine all ingredients in a blender.
2. Blend all ingredients until smoothie is thick and creamy.
3. Serve and enjoy!

NOTE:

- It is better to use frozen fruits for a rich, thicker and creamier texture.
- In case you do not have frozen fruits available, then add 1 cup of ice.
- Follow "Tips on How to Prepare a Smoothie (without dirtying your kitchen and spending extra time cleaning up" at the end of Chapter 2.

Chocolate Strawberry Protein Smoothie

Prep Time: 10 minutes
Serving: 1

Shopping List:

- ✓ Plant-based milk (i.e., almond, coconut)
- ✓ Frozen Strawberries
- ✓ Chocolate Protein Powder
- ✓ Cocoa Powder

Ingredients:

- 1 cup plant-based milk
- 1 cup strawberries, in halves & frozen
- 1 scoop of chocolate protein powder
- 1 tbsp cocoa powder

Directions:

1. Combine all ingredients in a blender.
2. Blend all ingredients until smoothie is thick and creamy.
3. Serve and enjoy!

NOTE:

- It is better to use frozen fruits for a rich, thicker and creamier texture.
- In case you do not have frozen fruits available, then add 1 cup of ice.
- Follow "Tips on How to Prepare a Smoothie (without dirtying your kitchen and spending extra time cleaning up" at the end of Chapter 2.

Chocolate Strawberry Banana Protein Smoothie

Prep Time: 10 minutes
Serving: 1

Shopping List:

- ✓ Plant-based milk (i.e., almond, coconut)
- ✓ Frozen Strawberries
- ✓ Frozen Banana
- ✓ Chocolate Protein Powder
- ✓ Cocoa Powder

Ingredients:

- 1 cup plant-based milk
- 1 cup strawberry, in halves & frozen
- 1 banana, frozen
- 1 scoop of chocolate protein powder
- 1 tbsp cocoa powder

Directions:

1. Combine all ingredients in a blender.
2. Blend all ingredients until smoothie is thick and creamy.
3. Serve and enjoy!

NOTE:

- It is better to use frozen fruits for a rich, thicker and creamier texture.
- In case you do not have frozen fruits available, then add 1 cup of ice.
- Follow "Tips on How to Prepare a Smoothie (without dirtying your kitchen and spending extra time cleaning up" at the end of Chapter 2.

Chocolate Avocado Protein Smoothie

Prep Time: 10 minutes
Serving: 1

Shopping List:

- ✓ Plant-based milk (i.e., almond, coconut)
- ✓ Frozen Avocado
- ✓ Chocolate Protein Powder
- ✓ Cocoa Powder

Ingredients:

- 1 cup plant-based milk (I use almond, coconut, or both)
- 1 avocado
- 1 scoop of chocolate protein powder
- 1 tbsp cocoa powder

Directions:

1. Combine all ingredients in a blender.
2. Blend all ingredients until smoothie is thick and creamy.
3. Serve and enjoy!

NOTE:

- It is better to use frozen fruits for a rich, thicker and creamier texture.
- In case you do not have frozen fruits available, then add 1 cup of ice.
- Follow "Tips on How to Prepare a Smoothie (without dirtying your kitchen and spending extra time cleaning up" at the end of Chapter 2.

Chocolate Mango Protein Smoothie

Prep Time: 10 minutes
Serving: 1

Shopping List:

- ✓ Plant-based milk (i.e., almond, coconut)
- ✓ Frozen Mango
- ✓ Chocolate Protein Powder
- ✓ Cocoa Powder

Ingredients:

- 1 cup plant-based milk (I use almond, coconut, or both)
- 1 mango, frozen
- 1 scoop of chocolate protein powder
- 1 tbsp cocoa powder

Directions:

1. Combine all ingredients in a blender.
2. Blend all ingredients until smoothie is thick and creamy.
3. Serve and enjoy!

NOTE:

- It is better to use frozen fruits for a rich, thicker and creamier texture.
- In case you do not have frozen fruits available, then add 1 cup of ice.
- Follow "Tips on How to Prepare a Smoothie (without dirtying your kitchen and spending extra time cleaning up" at the end of Chapter 2.

Chocolate Raspberry Protein Smoothie

Prep Time: 10 minutes
Serving: 1

Shopping List:

- ✓ Plant-based milk (i.e., almond, coconut)
- ✓ Frozen Raspberries
- ✓ Chocolate Protein Powder
- ✓ Cocoa Powder

Ingredients:

- 1 cup plant-based milk
- 1 cup raspberries
- 1 scoop of chocolate protein powder
- 1 tbsp cocoa powder

Directions:

1. Combine all ingredients in a blender.
2. Blend all ingredients until smoothie is thick and creamy.
3. Serve and enjoy!

NOTE:

- It is better to use frozen fruits for a rich, thicker and creamier texture.
- In case you do not have frozen fruits available, then add 1 cup of ice.
- Follow "Tips on How to Prepare a Smoothie (without dirtying your kitchen and spending extra time cleaning up" at the end of Chapter 2.

Chocolate Blueberry Protein Smoothie

Prep Time: 10 minutes
Serving: 1

Shopping List:

- ✓ Plant-based milk (i.e., almond, coconut)
- ✓ Frozen Blueberries
- ✓ Chocolate Protein Powder
- ✓ Cocoa Powder

Ingredients:

- 1 cup plant-based milk
- 1 cup blueberries, frozen
- 1 scoop of chocolate protein powder
- 1 tbsp cocoa powder

Directions:

1. Combine all ingredients in a blender.
2. Blend all ingredients until smoothie is thick and creamy.
3. Serve and enjoy!

NOTE:

- It is better to use frozen fruits for a rich, thicker and creamier texture.
- In case you do not have frozen fruits available, then add 1 cup of ice.
- Follow "Tips on How to Prepare a Smoothie (without dirtying your kitchen and spending extra time cleaning up" at the end of Chapter 2.

Chocolate Banana Protein Smoothie

Prep Time: 10 minutes
Serving: 1

Shopping List:

- ✓ Plant-based milk (i.e., almond, coconut)
- ✓ Frozen Banana
- ✓ Chocolate Protein Powder
- ✓ Cocoa Powder

Ingredients:

- 1 cup plant-based milk
- 1 banana, frozen
- 1 scoop of chocolate protein powder
- 1 tbsp cocoa powder

Directions:

1. Combine all ingredients in a blender.
2. Blend all ingredients until smoothie is thick and creamy.
3. Serve and enjoy!

NOTE:

- It is better to use frozen fruits for a rich, thicker and creamier texture.
- In case you do not have frozen fruits available, then add 1 cup of ice.
- Follow "Tips on How to Prepare a Smoothie (without dirtying your kitchen and spending extra time cleaning up" at the end of Chapter 2.

Chocolate Banana Mango Protein Smoothie

Prep Time: 10 minutes
Serving: 1

Shopping List:

- ✓ Plant-based milk (i.e., almond, coconut)
- ✓ Frozen Banana
- ✓ Frozen Mango
- ✓ Chocolate Protein Powder
- ✓ Cocoa Powder

Ingredients:

- 1 cup plant-based milk
- 1 banana, medium
- ½ mango
- 1 scoop of chocolate protein powder
- 1 tbsp cocoa powder

Directions:

1. Combine all ingredients in a blender.
2. Blend all ingredients until smoothie is thick and creamy.
3. Serve and enjoy!

NOTE:

- It is better to use frozen fruits for a rich, thicker and creamier texture.
- In case you do not have frozen fruits available, then add 1 cup of ice.
- Follow "Tips on How to Prepare a Smoothie (without dirtying your kitchen and spending extra time cleaning up" at the end of Chapter 2.

Chocolate Banana Mint Protein Smoothie

Prep Time: 10 minutes
Serving: 1

Shopping List:

- ✓ Plant-based milk (i.e., almond, coconut)
- ✓ Frozen Banana
- ✓ Mint Extract
- ✓ Chocolate Protein Powder
- ✓ Cocoa Powder

Ingredients:

- 1 cup plant-based milk
- 1 banana, medium
- ¼ tsp mint extract
- 1 scoop of chocolate protein powder
- 1 tbsp cocoa powder

Directions:

1. Combine all ingredients in a blender.
2. Blend all ingredients until smoothie is thick and creamy.
3. Serve and enjoy!

NOTE:

- It is better to use frozen fruits for a rich, thicker and creamier texture.
- In case you do not have frozen fruits available, then add 1 cup of ice.
- Follow "Tips on How to Prepare a Smoothie (without dirtying your kitchen and spending extra time cleaning up" at the end of Chapter 2.

Chocolate Mixed Berry Protein Smoothie

Prep Time: 10 minutes
Serving: 1

Shopping List:

- ✓ Plant-based milk (i.e., almond, coconut)
- ✓ Frozen Mixed Berries
- ✓ Chocolate Protein Powder
- ✓ Cocoa Powder

Ingredients:

- 1 cup plant-based milk
- 1 cup mixed berry
- 1 scoop of chocolate protein powder
- 1 tbsp cocoa powder

Directions:

1. Combine all ingredients in a blender.
2. Blend all ingredients until smoothie is thick and creamy.
3. Serve and enjoy!

NOTE:

- *Mixed berries consist of blueberries, strawberries, raspberries, & blackberries.*
- It is better to use frozen fruits for a rich, thicker and creamier texture.
- In case you do not have frozen fruits available, then add 1 cup of ice.
- Follow "Tips on How to Prepare a Smoothie (without dirtying your kitchen and spending extra time cleaning up" at the end of Chapter 2.

Chapter 5

Biggest Pitfalls of Smoothies

Smoothies are a healthy and versatile beverage that can be consumed as either a meal replacement, a pre- or post-workout drink, or a mid-morning or mid-afternoon snack. Yet, there are a few pitfalls that could sabotage the health benefits of smoothies. By not knowing these pitfalls, smoothies may not provide the health benefits necessary to improve your overall well-being.

1. Added Sugars

Added sugars reduce the nutrient density of these delicious beverages. Furthermore, routinely consuming too much added sugar may increase your risk of chronic ailments like heart disease, diabetes, and liver disease (Ld, 2020).

Yet, added sugars are difficult to avoid in our food intake. Thus, the American Heart Association (AHA) recommends to limit added sugar intake to no more than 9 teaspoons (36g) per day for men and 6 teaspoons (25g) per day for women (*Added Sugars*, 2024). Those added sugars are most found in commercially prepared and premade smoothies, which are found in grocery stores and supermarkets.

Potential sources of added sugars include the following: (Ld, 2020)

- Nut butters (e.g., peanut butter, almond butter)
- Protein powders
- Flavored yogurt
- Fruit-flavored sauces
- Sugar-sweetened juices
- Non-dairy milks

But you do not need to avoid added sugars all the time. It is important to limit their intake. I usually limit added sugars to less than 5g per high-protein smoothie. Here are some tips to limit added sugar intake when consuming a smoothie:

- *Use whole fruits to add sweetness to your smoothies instead of honey or maple syrup.*

- *If you really want that extra sweetness, limit the amount of honey or maple syrup you add.*

- *When looking for premade or commercially prepared smoothies, check the labels to ensure they contain little to no added sugars. Refer to the recommended added sugar intake guidelines from the American Heart Association.*

2. Protein Powders

Not all protein powders are created equal. While these powders consist of high amounts of protein, one of the ingredients that could sabotage a healthy smoothie is added sugar. As mentioned above, added sugar may lead to chronic health problems according to studies.

Protein powders are essential in making a high-protein smoothie and the added sugar issue can be resolved.

- *When choosing your favorite powder, go the Nutritional Fact label and look for Added Sugar under Carbohydrates. Check to make sure that there is little to no Added Sugar per scoop.*

I used *Sunwarrior Protein Warrior Blend*. They are made of organic ingredients and the added sugar is 1g. This protein powder has chocolate and vanilla flavors and is found in health stores and supermarkets. But feel free to pick any brand of protein powders. Just make sure the Added Sugar is little to none.

3. Nut Butters

As mentioned under the first pitfall, nut butters consist of Added Sugar too. However, not all nut butters have that ingredient. I love adding nut butter, such as peanut butter, to my smoothies. Here are my tips on how to add your favorite nut butter:

- *Once again, check the nutritional label for little to no Added Sugar.*

- *Choose powder version of the nut butter. The regular nut butters have more Added Sugar than powder version. I used PB2 Powder Peanut Powder which has 1g Added Sugar per 2 tablespoons compared to JIF Natural Creamy Peanut Butter spread, which has 2g Added Sugar per 2 tablespoons.*

- *If either you prefer regular nut butter or the powder version is not available in your area, cut down to 1 tablespoon nut butter instead of 2 tablespoons.*

TROUBLESHOOTING

Sometimes when making high-protein smoothies, the consistency and texture is not ideal. Either our smoothies end up too thick or too liquid. Here are a couple tips to address those issues:

- *If your smoothie is too thick, then add either more milk or water until the consistency is just right to your liking.*

- *If your smoothie is too liquid, either add more ice or add more fruit or vegetables until the consistency is just right to your liking.*

Conclusion

I hope you enjoyed these 30 recipes! By adding smoothies as part of my healthy regimen, my skin is healthier, I am more energetic, and my overall health improved.   These are just a few health benefits I have experienced, and I know you will experience those positive changes in your body and your overall mood too.

Incorporating these delicious and nutritious smoothies into your diet can be a game-changer for your health and wellbeing. Each recipe is crafted to not only satisfy your taste buds but also to provide you with essential nutrients and support your overall health goals.

Remember, the journey to better health is a continuous process, and every small step counts. Whether you're just starting out or looking to enhance your current habits, these smoothies offer a simple and enjoyable way to nourish your body.

Thank you so much for allowing me to share these recipes with you! And enjoy drinking your favorite smoothies!

If you enjoyed this smoothie recipe book, please follow me on Amazon Page.

And before you go,

Please leave an honest review!

References

Ld, A. H. R. (2020, May 11). *Are smoothies good for you?*
Healthline. https://www.healthline.com/nutrition/are-
smoothies-good-for-you

Quagliani, D., & Felt-Gunderson, P. (2016). Closing America's fiber
intake gap. *American Journal of Lifestyle Medicine*, *11*(1),
80–85. https://doi.org/10.1177/1559827615588079

LD, M. W. R. (2023, November 8). *How can antioxidants benefit
our health?* https://www.medicalnewstoday.com/articles/

Health Fitness Revolution. (2022, September 26). *10 reasons why
you should have a protein smoothie post workout.*
https://www.healthfitnessrevolution.com/10-reasons-why-
you-should-have-a-protein-smoothie-post-workout/

Juice Plus+. (2021, September 2). *How to preload your immune
system | Dr. Bill Sears | JPTV* [Video]. YouTube.
https://www.youtube.com/watch?v=AFAGBIR8WQk

Added sugars. (2024, May 22). www.heart.org. https://www.heart.org/en/healthy-living/healthy-eating/eat-smart/sugar/added-sugars

Made in United States
Troutdale, OR
12/02/2024

25688252R00040